CW00734089

Potty Training

Girls in 3 Days

A Modern Gentle and Positive Method

With a Continuation Plan

Nicole Rose

Download Your Free Gift Now

LEARN TO BUILD CONFIDENCE IN YOUR CHILDREN

As a way of saying "thank you" for your purchase,

I'm going to share with you a

Free Gift that is exclusive to readers of

Potty Training for Boys in 3 Days

It will provide you with the tools and guidance to know how to build up your children!

Click Here to Check it Out

CONTENTS

INTRODUCTION

As a parent, you might eagerly wait for your little girl to become more independent and use the potty without any effort. It is only normal to dream of getting rid of diapers, as these require a considerable financial investment.

Not surprisingly, toddlers have developed a serious attachment to their diapers, and they are not that prepared to give it up. Your daughter might refuse to be potty trained, but the solution is not to enter into a power struggle.

In this book, you will find a gentle and effective approach to potty training. Using our recommendations, it will be easier to support your daughter in her journey of independence. Working together toward a common goal, you will no longer give in to frustrations or experience anxiety.

Maybe you have already given potty training a try, without any result. Whether this is the case, or you are only now taking the first step, I want you to remember one thing. Potty training is challenging, and you need a clear plan to be successful. The stories coming from other parents might scare you, but each family has its own experience, and the three-day potty-training method will help you benefit from one that is positive.

I have written this book to help parents during one of the most challenging periods of their lives. By following this proven method, you will enjoy a stress-free experience, and you will be able to keep the risk of accidents down to a minimum.

Surely, it is not simple to go from zero to experienced in just three days. It will be a gruesome adventure but, hopefully, your little girl will finally say goodbye to diapers and concentrate on the potty. She will learn to acknowledge her bodily sensations and connect them to the potty, showing willingness and curiosity.

These three days might be long and tiring, and you will not have any "me time". Your toddler will require your complete attention, but it will all be worth it. Potty training will not only help you get rid of diapers; it will also represent a huge jump in your little girl's development.

As you will find out from the book, after the three-day period has come to an end, you will have to do a lot of maintenance. Little girls require time to integrate the new skills into their routine, and regressions are likely to occur. Do not worry, as I have included plenty of advice on how to handle these, as well as accidents.

It can be confusing to choose a specific potty-training method, as everyone seems to have a different opinion. I advise you to power through and choose the three-day potty-training approach and see what works best for your daughter. In the end, what matters is that you can help her achieve this new skill.

A potty-trained toddler will enjoy a renewed sense of independence, and you might also notice changes in her self-esteem and pride. That being said, I hope you will enjoy this book and recommend it to other parents as well. Are you ready for the training adventure?

CHAPTER 1

SIGNS OF READINESS

Getting rid of the diaper is an important objective for any parent. Naturally, you are eager to see your little girl coming into her independent self and using the potty without difficulties. Most children will achieve control around the age of 18 months and watching for signs of readiness ensures a better chance of success. Girls, however, might show signs of readiness slightly earlier than boys.

For your child to be able to use the toilet, there are two aspects to consider, meaning her physical abilities and emotional development. The age at which one is ready to learn this skill might differ, and you must be patient. It would be unrealistic to expect your toddler to stay dry when bladder control has not been achieved.

Is my child ready?

As parents, we often spend our time observing our children and the wonderful things they are doing. To determine if your daughter is ready, watch out for the following signs:

- *Ability to stay dry for at least two hours at a time* – some children manage to stay dry during the afternoon nap, or even throughout the entire night; there is a strong association with readiness and a reduction in the number of wet diapers

- *Acknowledges the need to wee or poop* – this is an important step, and one that will guarantee successful potty training; sensing the urge to go, some children will leave the room or even hide. Others will make a happy announcement, using either verbal communication or physical gestures.

- *Physical skills* – pulling pants up and down, getting on and off the potty, walking, etc.; it is also recommended that you facilitate this process, avoiding clothes that are difficult to take off. Kids might leave going to the potty until the last minute, so they need to be able to undress as quickly as possible.

- *Interest in toilet behavior* – children are great imitators, including when it comes to using the toilet; allow them to observe you, and you might soon see them copying your behavior

- *Ability to follow multi-step instructions* – it is always a good idea to wait until your little one has the ability to follow all the steps related to potty training. You can discuss the steps ahead, repeating the process several times. From noticing the urge to finding the bathroom and turning on the light, your child might require some time to get it right. Then will come the undressing, sitting on the potty, and peeing or pooping, followed by wiping and washing. Make sure your daughter presents both the willingness and ability to follow such instructions.

- *Ability to sit still* – this might not seem like an important thing, but it plays an essential role in the training process. Pooping in particular requires patience, so do what you can to facilitate your child's staying power. Books can be quite helpful in that department.

- *Desire to use the potty* – if your child shows interest in using the potty, that is great; she might also want to wear big girl undies, or tell you how she likes doing the same things you do ("like mommy"). You can take advantage of this desire, modeling the behavior and presenting your daughter with books or videos on the subject. Talk about going to the potty and offer words of encouragement.

- *Showing independence* – your little one might surprise you with words such as "I can do it myself", and you should support the desire to be independent; such ambition guarantees a higher rate of success

- *Soiled diapers make her feel uncomfortable* – upon reaching the corresponding developmental age, children may no longer appreciate a soiled diaper and they will ask to be changed or even to use the potty

- *Predictable bowel movements* – by a certain age, you might notice a predictable schedule with regard to pooping; some children poop in the morning, while others do it after eating – knowing the order of business, it might be easier to redirect your little one to the potty.

Should I wait?

Sometimes, it might obvious that it is not the right time to start potty training. For instance, when a significant change has occurred, it might be for the best to wait. This can include moving into a new home, welcoming another baby, or starting daycare.

It can also happen that your little one feels overwhelmed at having to learn such a complex skill, returning to the babyhood period for comfort. Have patience and wait until she is ready to try, without pressuring her into giving up the diaper. You will notice the moment your child has become aware of her bodily functions, being prepared to give the potty a try.

CHAPTER 2

POTTY TRAINING A GIRL

Are girls easier to potty train than boys? There is no right answer to this question. However, we must acknowledge the differences between genders and adjust our efforts accordingly. As mentioned in the previous chapter, girls might be willing to start the training process at a younger age.

Reasons for early potty training success

Why the difference? It seems that they can achieve control faster, with fewer accidents during sleep. Their communication skills develop at an accelerated rate, so they can share the need to go without difficulties. It is also a known fact that girls have better concentration abilities, being able to sit still for longer periods of time.

Given their developmental advance, it should come as no surprise girls achieve control faster. They also need a shorter timeframe to achieve potty training, as opposed to boys, who might need additional tries. For a girl, the process might be easier, as she can sit down for both peeing and pooping. Boys have it harder, as they must master two different processes, but they too can start sitting down for both.

Girls like to be involved in the process

You can ensure the success of the training by involving your little princess in the decision-making process. For instance, you can let her choose the big girl pants – she will love seeing her favorite characters on them. The trick is to buy underwear that is simply too pretty to ruin; many little girls enjoy beautiful undies, and they will want to stay dry, instead of soiling their new purchases.

You might also go out together and purchase a cute potty, as well as books on the subject. If you make the whole experience seem fun, she will appreciate your efforts and respond in the way you desire. For little girls who are not thrilled about wiping, toilet paper with fun prints might be an excellent idea.

Teach her how to wipe

This is an essential skill to teach your daughter. You have to make sure she wipes correctly, otherwise, she might develop urinary infections. The correct way to do it is front to back, and not back to front – you have to avoid spreading the bacteria from her bowels to the vagina and urethra.

Urinary tract infections are more common in girls than boys, and it is important to be aware of the symptoms that might appear. You might notice that your little girl asks to pee more often, having a hard time holding on. Peeing can be painful, and she might also complain of a tummy ache. Accidents are more frequent during periods of infection.

It can be hard for your daughter to understand the process, especially when pooping is involved. For this reason, you might consider splitting the wiping training into steps. Teach her to pat herself dry after peeing, and keep on wiping her bottom until she makes the connection. It's no use rushing the process but don't forget to remind her why she has to follow the same steps every time.

Help her learn about bodily functions

Toddlers are famous for their eagerness to learn. They absorb new information like a sponge, and parents should take advantage of this hunger, including when it comes to potty training. You can read potty books together, watch educational videos, and talk about what happens in our bodies and how we need to eliminate waste.

As previously mentioned, learning by imitation delivers the best chances for success. Keep the door to the bathroom open and allow your daughter to notice how you are sitting down to use the toilet. At the same time, she will see that her daddy stands up to pee, and you will have the opportunity to explain a few basic differences between genders.

Discuss cleanliness

You might also discuss the importance of cleanliness, and how we need to protect ourselves against infections. Always use age-appropriate terms, but make sure to take advantage of your daughter's innate desire for staying clean. Present the potty as the cleaner option, and remind her that big girls do not like soiled diapers.

Pretend play as practice

What do little girls like to do most in the world? Play. Their imagination knows no limits, and they will always invent their own games to have fun. Don't ignore this unlimited creativity, and use it to introduce the potty. You can use dolls or stuffed animals, resorting to pretend play to reinforce toilet behavior and healthy habits. The play sessions will also offer excellent opportunities on what not to do, so you should give them a try.

Watch out for the signs that she needs to go

With the potty training process in full development, you have to pay attention to your little girl and notice signs of an emergency. Remember she is learning to control her bodily functions, and accidents can occur, especially if she doesn't reach the potty in time.

All kids, not only girls, can get preoccupied with other activities, leaving the peeing or pooping for the last minute. You might notice your daughter, during play, how she hops from one foot to the other, wriggling her entire body. Some girls hold their hands between their legs, fighting the urge to go.

CHAPTER 3

THE 3-DAY POTTY TRAINING METHOD

Preparation

Start the process with plenty of patience and take things step-by-step. You want to introduce your child to the potty in a manner that is both casual and playful, without causing her to become anxious. Children are guided by instinct and it is natural for them to offer resistance with each significant change; our reassurance is necessary, so they can ease into the transition process and finally get rid of the diaper.

Presenting the potty

Take out the potty and talk to your daughter about it, and the purpose its serves. You can place it in the bathroom, as this will help her make the right association, and allow exploration without limits. Some children like to sit on the potty fully dressed, pretending they are either peeing or pooping – this is great, as it means you have already taken a step in the right direction.

Allow your daughter to get used to the potty

For children, change is difficult. They are treading on unknown territory, fearing what lies ahead. Even though you might be eager for your little one to get undressed and sit on the potty, using it as intended, remind yourself this is not an easy process. Have patience and allow your daughter to get used to the potty, so it does not feel foreign anymore.

Model toilet behavior

Once again, this is part of the preparation period, and it can help your daughter understand bodily functions and how girls eliminate waste. You can take her to the bathroom and allow her to observe you, as well as engage in discussions about peeing and pooping. Use language she can understand, and get her to ask questions, as your answers will shed even more light on the matter.

Books about the potty

You might not realize it, but the books written on the subject of potty training can be lifesavers. Children can learn a lot from stories presenting familiar situations, and they might find it easier to relate to characters who are going through the same things as them. The good news is that there are plenty of books available on using the potty, so you will have from where to choose.

Poop and pee go into the potty

Do not expect little kids to understand this from the first attempt. You have to repeatedly remind them that poop and pee go into the potty, and not into the diaper or on the floor. To illustrate the process, you might empty a poopy diaper into the toilet.

Keep in mind that your daughter has learned to poop in the diaper, so it is naturally hard for her to form a different association. Show her how things stand, and how important it is for us to use the potty.

Dress for success

Do not dress your little girl in fancy dresses or complicated outfits, or you can expect more accidents to follow. Avoid clothes with too many buttons or layers, as they will only get in the way and reduce the chances of success. The right clothes, such as pants that pull up and down easily, will ensure the desired potty victory.

During the potty-training process, some parents decide to leave their toddlers naked or half-naked. In this way, they become more aware of the signals their body send, and the risk of accidents is significantly lower. After all, it is easier to rush to the potty with a naked toddler, instead of having to go through overalls or other similar outfits.

Treat resistance with patience and perseverance

It can very well happen that your little girl refuses to welcome the potty, showing resistance to the training process. Using two essential weapons – patience and perseverance – create an environment in which she will feel supported to take the next step. Teach her about the body and how it functions, introducing important words to remember (body parts, bodily functions, etc.).

Don't fight with your daughter, as this is not the way to convince any child to accept change. Offer your support and take your time in preparing for the training process, finding a way to say goodbye to diapers. For instance, you might encourage her to give away her remaining diapers to another family, who has children younger of age.

Let's talk about it

Just because your daughter is only a toddler, this doesn't mean you should disregard her feelings. Ask her how she feels, and offer your unconditional love. Take her through the entire process and explain what is going to happen.

Make a point of proving how thrilled you are to have a big girl, who is eager to learn all these new skills. Children thrive when they see their parents being proud of them, even if such feelings are related to something as mundane as going to the potty.

It might also be important for you to mention everyone has bodily functions, and how we must pay attention to the signals our bodies send. If you have pets, you can draw an association from there and explain how they eliminate waste. Whatever you do, refrain from using negative language, otherwise your little one might refuse the training altogether.

Prepare yourself for the challenges ahead

Seeing your little girl grow up can be sweet and difficult at the same time. Using the potty means a new chapter in your life, one that will include plenty of challenges but also a big benefit at the end: an independent toddler, who no longer relies on you to peep and/or poop. Prepare yourself for the challenges ahead, and you might find it easier to go through the entire process.

Things you need

It is a good idea to go into battle prepared, stocking up with everything that might be necessary for potty training success. You can organize your shopping list per the suggestions presented below.

Potty/adapter seat

Nowadays, little girls have a wide range of choices in terms of potties. The potty is a practical choice, as it will allow your daughter to feel more secure, as opposed to a large toilet. Naturally, this is also the safer alternative. A travel potty is a good investment for the future, so make sure to add it to your list.

The child-size potty is easily accepted by toddlers, especially if you allow them to personalize it. You can apply stickers on the potty together, and this activity will make it seem less scary. The trick is to lessen any anxiety that might interfere with potty training.

Some parents prefer using an adapter seat for the toilet, and that is perfectly fine. If you decide to go with this option, make sure the seat is secure and comfortable. A stool might be necessary to facilitate your child's independence, and also to help with bowel movements.

Learning tools/supplies

The better prepared you are, the higher your chance of success is going to be. Your list should include toilet training books that are specific for girls, as well as stickers, reward charts, and dolls or stuffed animals to practice. Think of these supplies are learning tools – you need them to support your daughter in making the transition from diaper to big girl pants.

Clothes & accessories

It is normal for your toddler to view the potty training experience as something difficult. This is the reason why you need to make things as easy as possible, including when it comes to clothes.

Prepare yourself several outfits, opting for loose-fitting garments. The pants should be simple to pull down and back up. If you decide to leave your child half-naked, then you should stock up on knee socks and/or leg warmers.

Underwear

The right underwear can help your daughter feel more comfortable about the big change. As proposed, choose undies with her favorite characters or popping designs. You can let her choose – she will enjoy the freedom of choice, showing care in not ruining her new undies.

Extra sheets & absorbent pads

Accidents are bound to happen as your little one leaves the diaper behind. It is a good idea to prepare a few extra sheets, as well as purchase several absorbent pads. These can reduce the damage caused by a nap or nighttime accidents. All you have to do is place them under your child's sheet.

Cleaning products

Given the obvious risk of accidents, it does not hurt to be prepared in this department as well. Stock up on cleaning products and you won't be sorry, especially when you will have to clean up one mishap after the other. Be sure to purchase disinfecting substances as well, as these can help your toddler stay safe and healthy.

Age-appropriate games

Toddlers do not like being cooped inside the house. They go bored easily, and boredom often leads to imaginative attempts. To survive the three days of intense potty training, prepare yourself with various age-appropriate games. If you have to spend so much time together, it might help to look at this period as an opportunity to introduce your daughter to new experiences and/or activities.

Food & beverages

Your shopping list should include food and beverages for three days. To save time, you might prep your meals ahead of time. Do not forget to purchase salty snacks, as these cause thirst, causing your toddler to drink more fluids and use the potty more often.

In terms of beverages, stick to water and diluted fruit juice. You might also want to offer popsicles or pieces of fruits that rich in water. Encourage your daughter to drink plenty of fluids, without exaggerating.

Fun rewards

Toddlers respond magnificently to positive reinforcement, and the right reward will ensure a smoother path toward toilet independence. Food can be used as a treat, but other great alternatives should be considered. You can set a reward chart and use stickers to praise your daughter for her achievements.

Concerns

Just like your toddler, you are treading on an unknown territory as well. You might feel afraid that you are pushing your little one, feeling it hard to say goodbye to her babyhood. Do not fret, as each period in your daughter's life is beautiful, and you can overcome any concerns together.

Should I let her watch and learn?

Even though you might crave intimacy when using the toilet, it can help your toddler to observe you. Imitation allows them to learn, including in this department. Think of the observation process as a natural first step, and let her watch you from time to time.

As you are not the only adult inside the house, your daughter might notice that her daddy or sibling pee standing up. This is an excellent opportunity for teaching her about gender differences. If she attempts to imitate them, explain how girls have to sit down to pee. Your effort might be met by resistance, so refrain from engaging in a power struggle.

How should I refer to body parts?

Parents are often tempted to use cutesy words for genitals, thinking their toddlers are too small for the actual terms. However, when we avoid using the right words, we are sending our daughters the wrong message. It is not a shame to talk about our body parts, and we should not look at the experience as something embarrassing.

Does pressuring her yield better results?

The three-day training period is obviously intense, and you will have to display a lot of patience. Keep in mind that your toddler might have a hard time adjusting to the new set of demands, so it is no use to add even more pressure.

Make sure you understand the difference between motivation and pressure. While it is perfectly fine to motivate your daughter in achieving these new skills, pressuring her will not yield better results. On the contrary, she might become defiant and refuse to use the potty altogether.

How does naked time help?

Yes, naked time helps, and quite a lot. As mentioned above, it can help your daughter become more sensitive to the signals her body sends. Whether you decide to dress only the upper body or leave her completely naked, she will require less time to figure out that she needs to go.

Be there for her, and do your best to watch for signs that she needs to use the potty. As a general rule, the more time she will spend out of the diaper, the better her chances of learning this skill within the allocated three-day period.

Is it wrong to take a break?

Are you familiar with the motto: "if at first, you don't succeed, try again"? Well, with toddlers, things are often unpredictable. Taking a break does not hurt, and it might even reduce the risk of accidents. Whatever happens, refrain from overreacting or punishing your little one. It's no use to make her feel bad; instead, make sure to remind her that accidents are normal, and part of the training process. Breaks allow you to dissipate the frustration and return to a calm, peaceful atmosphere, yielding better results in the end.

Constipation, a potential risk

Constipation is indeed a risk with newly-trained toddlers. While peeing is definitely a simpler experience, pooping might be a hard concept to grasp. In the beginning, they might abstain from having a bowel movement – if you allow this behavior to persist, constipation can occur.

The solution is to encourage your little girl, and praise her for each potty success. Once again, you can resort to books or videos to explain that poop goes into the potty, and there is no reason to be frightened or ashamed. During the training period, you might also want to avoid foods that can lead to constipation, offering plenty of water and fiber-rich fruits or vegetables.

Day 1

The first day is always the hardest, but you have to maintain your composure and be there for your little girl. In the morning, you can recap the discussion on saying goodbye to diapers, at least during awake time. Some parents continue to use diapers for naps and night sleep.

Everyone in the family should be involved in the process, not only your spouse but also any other caregivers. In this way, your daughter will learn using the potty is not something to be achieved only in the presence of a particular adult. She will also understand this is connected to her physiological needs, not to specific situations or people.

So, are you ready? First thing you should change your daughter out of her diaper. You can then decide whether she should wear clothes or spend her day half-naked; the decision is yours, of course, but a bare bottom will help her become more aware of the need to go. Both diapers and underpants can hinder such sensations, not to mention they defeat the whole purpose of potty training.

Show your little one where the potty is, and make sure to draw attention to the fact that both pee and poop go in there. You can keep a potty in the bathroom, and another one in the living room for easier access. Once again, this is your decision, but you should keep in mind your daughter is only discovering her bodily sensations and a trip to the bathroom might prove out to be too long.

Throughout the day, encourage your daughter to drink a lot of fluids, sticking to water, diluted fruit juice, or milk. You want your child to pee frequently, as each potty visit means a reinforcement of the desired behavior. A sippy cup can help you stick to your schedule, so make sure it is within reach. Do not wait for your daughter to communicate the need to go; try to anticipate it, watching for obvious signs.

Is she exhibiting a clear need to go? Do not wait. Take her immediately to the potty, otherwise, you might soon have an accident to clean up after. Even if she does not present any signs, it is still a good idea to ask her if she needs to go. You set a timer and ask the question every half an hour. In this way, you will create a habit, and help your daughter make the connection between bodily sensations and using the potty.

If your daughter refuses to try, do not lose your calm. Instead, offer her the opportunity to try again, perhaps after she is done playing. A good strategy is to get her on the potty after every main activity of the day – when she wakes up in the morning or after her afternoon nap, before and after meals, before bedtime, and so on. You want to integrate the potty training experience into her daily routine.

As a parent, you cannot help but interpret your child's behavior from an emotional point of view. During the first day, you might have to face a lot of refusals, accidents, and cleanups. Find a way to remain objective and refrain from criticizing your daughter. Remind her she now has to pee/poop in the potty. If an accident has occurred, do not use harsh words; you might ask her to help you clean up instead.

You are raising a tiny human, who still has to understand how the world works. Using the potty might seem like a simple thing to you, but not the same thing can be said about your daughter. She might find it hard to go through her first day, so make sure to reward the progress she's made. You can use encouraging phrases, as well as a reward chart – she will love receiving stickers for each potty success.

If your little one has a shy personality, she might not like to be the center of attention. Be her source of comfort and allow her to take breaks from the training process, especially if she is overwhelmed. In deciding how the day will unfold, always consider your child's needs.

Helpful suggestions to get through the first day easier

- You can allow your daughter to stay completely naked if you want, but make sure your house is warm and she wears at least socks or knee-warmers

- Do not force high quantities of fluid, especially fruit juice, as this can lead to discomforting symptoms (diarrhea)

- Teach her to wash her hands after each potty use, using the experience as a learning opportunity (reinforcement of healthy habits)

- Practice potty training with a doll, using the same words or phrases to reinforce toilet habits

- Don't go back to diapers, no matter how tempting this may sound – you are making progress, even if it does not feel like it.

Day 2

It might feel like you are doing the same thing over and over again, with minimal results. Welcome to the second day of potty training, where you will repeat everything from the previous day.

By now, you have probably gotten an idea of how the whole experience is going to turn out. If your little girl still has a lot of accidents, it might be best to stay inside and work on improving the training routine. On the other hand, if you have been successful, you can choose to go outside for a brief period.

Going out with a child who is not fully-trained can present several challenges. However, with a few careful measures, you can make the experience fun and reduce possible mishaps. The first recommendation is to take short walks around the house or visit a nearby playground. Always carry a portable potty and use absorbent pads for car travels.

Whether you like it or not, accidents can occur. Your daughter might become so preoccupied with playing, that she will forget to announce the need to go. Carry a change of underwear and do not use harsh words or make her feel ashamed for what has happened. Remember, kids are sensitive and we do not want to crush their spirit.

To keep the risk of accidents down to a minimum, you should dress her in loose clothes, with no underwear. Just like inside the house, this will help her realize she needs to go. Nonetheless, if she has displayed excellent control the previous day, you might revisit the issue. Potty training is not an exact science, and each parent can observe her child and decide on the best way to go.

Throughout the second day, watch for signs that she needs to go and use positive reinforcement to encourage correct behavior. You might still offer a high quantity of fluids, as frequent bathroom trips will solidify the learning experience. Ask your daughter if she needs to go at regular intervals – do not leave it all to her, as kids are easily distracted. Stick to your schedule and use specific words to remind her of proper bathroom etiquette.

No matter how difficult it might be, try not to lose your patience. You do not want to hurry your daughter or force her into achieving complete control before she is ready. Instead, you should encourage your little girl to visit the potty as often as possible and maintain a positive attitude.

Helpful suggestions to get through the second day easier

- Use praise and positive reinforcement to stimulate your daughter's interest in using the potty

- Assess her progress before deciding whether she should remain half-naked, naked, or wear loose-fitting clothes

- Help her become more independent by encouraging her to wipe herself and wash her hands after each potty use

- Practice makes perfect – offer her as many learning opportunities as possible

- Talk about the potty and how it feels to be a big girl, kids need to discuss their feelings and work on understanding them.

Day 3

After a lot of trial and error, you have arrived at the last day of the intense potty training experience. This is the day to reinforce bathroom etiquette, preparing your little girl for the days lying ahead.

Keep on reminding about the need to go, as the repetition will only help your daughter become more familiar with her own bodily sensations. At this point, and following the progress she's made, you can decide whether to eliminate the diaper during naps/bedtime. Some children require a longer period to attain control, and there should be no rush in that department.

You have probably noticed the progress yourself. Some kids even wake up dry, leaving their parents amazed. The more your daughter gains experience, the less stressed you are. The number of accidents has probably reduced, and you have gotten used to offering positive reinforcement round the clock.

The routine you have now will have to be maintained after these three days until you are certain that your little one has mastered bathroom etiquette. A well-structured schedule will only lead to further learning and development, so do not stray away from what you have achieved. Remember to avoid harsh words and criticism, and to watch your own behavior, as kids are expert imitators.

On the third day, you can consider a longer outing. Depending on your child's control, you might travel by car or do an activity at a considerable distance from home. As with previous outings, you should carry a travel potty, as well as a change of clothes, wipes, and sanitizer. Very few children accept going to a public restroom, so do not make any assumptions. It is for the best to be prepared, so you can handle any accident in a matter of minutes.

Helpful suggestions to get through the third day easier

- Go cold turkey and eliminate diapers for naps and bedtime only if your child has exhibited clear signs of control

- Keep on offering praise and positive reinforcement – kids always need to feel supported, even when they begin to manage something by themselves

- Offer to take them to the potty at regular intervals, but make sure the time period is bigger by day three

- Do not be disappointed if your daughter still has accidents – each child progresses at her own level and you must be patient

- A relaxed attitude offers better results than forcefulness, and kind words offer encouragement, as opposed to criticism.

Reflect on how these three days have been, and the progress your little one has achieved. You might go through a period of intense changes, but they all contribute to a child who is smarter and more independent.

CHAPTER 4

NAPS VS. BEDTIME

Reaching the point where your daughter is 100% diaper-free can be challenging, especially since you have to factor in both naps and night sleep. In deciding how you are going to proceed, you might also want to consider the progress your little one has made.

All or nothing – what is the best approach?

Some parents prefer to focus on daytime training, continuing to use diapers or pull-up undies for sleep. While it is true that such an approach is easier, it can also be disorienting. Your little girl might insist to wear the diaper even though she is awake, and you have to be firm. Remind her the diaper/pull-offs are used only for sleep, and she should always announce the need to go.

If you are going to give up diapers altogether, it might be less confusing but you should expect more accidents. During the day, children learn to make the association between their physiological needs and using the potty. However, when it comes to sleep, the issue is a bit more complicated.

Even though children might exhibit obvious signs of readiness, they will need additional time to reach full control. Accidents occur because the brain has not made the association between waking up and going to the potty; you have to be patient and wait until your daughter attains the necessary skills. The nighttime training can last between a few days and several weeks, but there are exceptions. Some kids stay dry throughout the entire night from the start.

Handle accidents with patience and calm

You might be utterly impressed with your daughter's progress during the day. However, come nighttime, accidents might happen with increased frequency. Night training takes more time and you have to be prepared. You cannot expect your little one to stay dry all at once, especially if she has one or two accidents when she is awake.

Yes, it can be frustrating to watch over a sleeping toddler, hoping she will manage to keep dry. Her brain is working on acknowledging the need to go at night, so you have to be patient. If your daughter is a deep sleeper, the matter might be even harder to handle. If an accident has occurred, do not overreact; change the sheets and her clothes, and help her go back to sleep.

Work on your bedtime routine

Each night, before going to sleep, put your little one on the potty. Explain to her she needs to go, so she won't have any accidents during the night. Work on developing a bedtime routine, and you will reap the benefits over time.

Your daughter might want to drink plenty of fluids before going to bed, but you have to stand your ground and refuse. Once again, you have to talk to your little girl and point out the fact that accidents are bound to happen. If she drinks a lot of water, she will either end up peeing in the bed or wake up to use the potty – both options are not at all appealing for a toddler.

It cannot hurt to be prepared, so stock up on absorbent pads and underwear or pull-offs. If you are planning on using diapers, keep a few by the bed for easy access. After the three-day training period, you have probably noticed a pattern of behaviors and you already know if your daughter can stay dry or not.

Signs of progress

If your little girl wakes up during the night and asks to use the potty, you have made progress. Naturally, it is frustrating to wake up and take her to the toilet, but in a few days, this will become part of your routine.

Acknowledging a wet diaper is another sign you are moving forward. Your daughter has become aware of the discomfort a wet or dirty diaper creates, and soon, she might wake up dry, as the brain has registered the unpleasant association.

CHAPTER 5

LONG-TERM PLAN OF ACTION

Just because the three days are over, this doesn't mean you should stop working toward achieving full bladder and bowel control. The main idea is to get rid of diapers for good, keeping accidents down to a minimum.

Take a moment to think about how the training experience was, and assess your daughter's progress. Compare the frequency of potty uses versus the number of accidents, and try to identify potential challenges.

Plan of action for long-term success

To ensure the desired long-term success, you will have to consider various aspects. The list below will help you formulate the best plan of action for your daughter.

- Ask her if she needs to go – kids are easily distracted, and three days are not enough to embed awareness deep in her brain; so, keep asking, and you will not have to worry as much about accidents.

- Naked or dressed – you are free to decide, in accordance to how well the three days of training unfolded; you can continue with the bare bottom or use loose-fitting clothes, with underwear optional. Remember that undies can still remind her of the diaper, increasing the risk of mishaps.

- Calmness and reassurance – these are two attributes you will need to develop, particularly if you want to avoid regressions. Even when your daughter has woken up dry, with few or no accidents during the day, she might still find going to the potty to be a scary experience. Offer your reassurance and stay calm in case she makes a mistake.

- Daycare plan – as your daughter will go to daycare, it is essential to talk with the teacher and establish a common plan. The goal is to prevent accidents and avoid going back to diapers; luckily, teachers are often interested in independence, being more than pleased to reinforce the newly-learned lessons.

- All caregivers involved – everyone should be on the same page, encouraging your little girl to use the potty and communicate the need to go. You can work together and reinforce bathroom etiquette, using the same words and gestures.

- Stick to your routine – slowly, you will get back to normal, but this does not mean you should forget all about potty training. Find a way to incorporate the practice into your daily schedule, offering as many learning opportunities as possible.

- Long trips with all the essentials – the good news is that you can dare to take longer trips, as long as you are adequately prepared. Choose locations equipped with bathrooms or carry a portable potty in the trunk of your car. Take a change of clothes and several sets of underwear.

- Encouragement is key – encourage your little girl to use the potty, gradually increasing the interval between uses. Over time, you will notice she has become more confident, exhibiting excellent control.

- Kindness goes a long way – speak to your daughter in a kind manner, and praise her for staying dry. If accidents still occur, watch your words, as you do not want to add to the hurt she is already experiencing.

How to handle potty training regression

Regression can occur at any moment, and to solve it, you must first find out what led to it. Below, you will find a couple of useful suggestions on how to handle potty training regression effectively and get your daughter back on the right track.

- Acknowledge the effect of major changes – starting daycare, moving into a new home, welcoming another baby – all of these things can cause your little girl to feel uncertain, wanting to go back to old habits.

- Stand your ground in case of power struggles – sometimes, the potty training regression is nothing more but a power struggle. Your toddler wants to feel in control, having chosen the potty to dominate the situation. Take a step back and point out the obvious – going to the potty is a physiological need, and she will have to pee eventually.

- Self-doubt & low level of confidence – young children might exhibit a significant fear of failure, preferring to quit when the going gets tough. As her parent, you need to do whatever it takes and help your daughter overcome her fears.

- Not enough attention – when children feel overlooked, they begin to act out with the hope their parents will pay more attention to them. Instead of giving in to frustration, make an effort and find more time to spend together, doing the things she likes.

- Emotional immaturity – toddlers are still learning how to control their emotions, often resorting to crying and clinginess to express themselves. To avoid regression and accidents, you have to stay calm and exhibit patience.

- Revenge – you might not expect your daughter to be vengeful, but it can happen. To solve the situation and get things back to normal, talk to her and ask about potential reasons. The answer might surprise you.

There is no magic recipe to handling regressions, but it is clear our little girls need kindness and patience, first and foremost. Say no to anger and threats, and do not give in to her demands, no matter how persistent she might be. Enforce age-appropriate consequences when needed and base your actions on her motivation, rather than potential rewards. Offer your attention and love, and make sure each use of the potty transforms into a learning opportunity.

CHAPTER 6

FREQUENTLY ASKED QUESTIONS & ANSWERS

Does this method truly deliver?

The answer is yes. Your daughter might respond to the training, and learn how to use the potty in just three days. However, I would like to point out that every child is different, and in some cases, it might take a bit longer. Several factors are influencing the end-result, including the home environment and parenting skills. Be patient and help your little girl get there.

How hard will this be?

By now, you have probably understood this is an intense training program. You should expect it to be hard, not only for your daughter but also for you. There are three days in which you will be mostly confined to your house, and your toddler will get bored.

You might feel defeated and tempted to quit. I advise you to power through and encourage your little one to use the potty. Months later, you will look back, and you will be happy for having decided to go on. To ease the process and increase your chances of success, include everyone in the training process.

Will we have many accidents?

That depends, of course, on each child and the progress she is making. On the first day, as mentioned, you should expect a higher frequency of accidents. However, their number should reduce on the following days.

You should remember, though, that your daughter needs time to associate bodily sensations with the actual use of the potty. Patience is key and you might want to use each accident as a learning opportunity. Never scold or shame your child for not being able to hold it in, as this will only shed a negative light on potty training.

What if my child is stubborn?

Many parents wonder if this method works on stubborn children. Once again, the answer is yes. You are training their brain to acknowledge the need to go and connect it to using the potty. Their stubbornness might make the process more difficult, but not impossible.

For young kids, everything is a power struggle. If your daughter frequently refuses to go to the potty, I recommend taking a break and trying again after a few days. Do not make empty threats, as these will only lead to even more obstinacy. Show empathy instead and try to talk to your little girl about her feelings.

Why am I not successful?

We all want our children to become more independent. At the toddler stage, potty training is a big deal, as getting rid of the diaper would make everything easier. However, it is never a good idea to pressure them into achieving control before they are ready.

Wrapped in our emotions, we might find it hard to stay positive. Instead, we will scold and punish our little ones, often turning towards negative reinforcements. Kids have feelings as well, and they will never respond to such behavior. On the contrary, they might refuse to use the potty altogether.

If you are not making headway, you might want to take a moment and consider your approach. To be successful, you have to maintain a positive attitude, and turn potty training into a fun activity. Use praise and adequate rewards, and be there for your daughter, especially if she has a hard time adjusting to life without a diaper.

Why does poop training take longer?

Children need to reach a certain developmental age to achieve bowel control. They might feel comfortable with pooping in the diaper while using the potty or the toilet terrifies them. You have to show your support and be understanding, doing everything necessary to attenuate your daughter's discomfort.

You do not want to scar your little one, causing her to be so scared that she will refuse to poop. A positive mindset will be beneficial during the training process – you need to encourage her to poop in the potty and celebrate each success. Once she will feel comfortable, she won't have any issues with using the potty.

Yelling or shaming often ruin the progress a child has made. As the parent, you have to teach your daughter that pooping in the potty is the logical thing to do. Take your time to explain to her nothing bad will happen, and that her body can handle the whole process. Offer your support and read books on pooping. There are also plenty of educational videos you can use to enrich the learning experience.

What do I do if my daughter refuses to use a public restroom?

Most kids are terrified of public restrooms, so refusal is pretty much a given thing. Try to be understanding and walk your little one through the process. Show her how the toilet works, and offer assurance she won't fall in. You can let her watch you use the toilet, and also explain she has no alternative, other than wetting her pants.

It might be a good idea to turn the whole activity into a game, as this will help your little girl overcome her fears and concentrate on the fun part. Once you convince her to use the toilet, make sure to not let the automatic flush set off. Cover the sensor, as most kids hate the unexpected sound a toilet makes. Their brain will register the unpleasant experience, reinforcing the need for refusal.

How to prevent accidents while traveling?

Traveling with a toddler is a complicated experience, but you can make things easier by preparing ahead. Go shopping with your daughter and choose a fun portable potty, storing it in the car in case of emergencies. There are also little bags you can purchase for pooping, you can place these in the potty and, thus, clean up within minutes.

Many parents are worried about the car seat being ruined in case of an accident. Until you are certain that your daughter can hold it in, especially over a significant distance, you can place one of those absorbent pads on the car seat. Always make sure you have a spare change of clothes in your car for such cases.

CHAPTER 7

POTTY TRAINING PRAISE AND ENCOURAGEMENT

Offering the right words of encouragement can help your little girl feel less scared, and more inclined to use the potty as instructed. In training a child to achieve control, you must always maintain a positive and gentle approach, with plenty of praise.

As parents, we become accustomed to encouraging our little ones to do various things and thus achieve new abilities or skills. With potty training, things are not as different and our main goal should be complete cooperation. Words can pave the way toward success, but we should always pay attention to our child's personality before using certain phrases.

Timid

A timid child might require a longer timeline to adjust to significant changes, such as using the potty. Too much praise might make her feel uncomfortable or pressured. If you see her overwhelmed, give her space and take a break from the training process.

Encouraging phrases:

"You did a nice job using the potty"

"I liked how you washed your hands"

"Mommy is proud of you"

Independent

Children with independent personalities might enjoy using the potty, feeling motivated by the freedom it brings. Words can help them become even more motivated, and they will certainly take delight in your praise.

Encouraging phrases:

"You did a good job peeing in the potty"

"Way to go! You managed to wipe yourself"

"I liked how well you washed your hands, with no help"

Obliging

If your child is eager to please, using the potty should not be a problem. Your daughter will respond well to praise, especially if you will take the time to mention specific things she did well.

Encouraging phrases:

"Way to go! You managed to pull down your pants, just like mommy"

"Mommy is proud of how you said goodbye to the diapers"

"Great job washing your hands just like I showed you"

Prudent

As the mother of a prudent toddler, you are probably aware of how important it is to them for their progress to be acknowledged.

With potty training, you can use a reward chart, letting your little girl apply stickers for each achievement. Aside from that, she will expect you to offer praise and encouragement.

Encouraging phrases:

"Great job, you have used the potty for both pee and poop today"

"Way to go! You deserve a sticker for how great you did today"

"I am so proud you waited to pee or poop in the potty!"

Spirited

Praise is something an active child will never say no to. However, it might take some time before you will discover what kind of words your child responds to. In choosing your verbal praise, make sure you target the desired behavior.

"Way to go! You had no accidents today, and you deserve a treat!"

"I am so proud you managed to poop in the potty, you are a big girl now"

"Mommy loved how you stop playing to use the potty, that was so smart of you"

What happens if your little one has an accident? We have to keep ourselves in check and refrain from scolding or shaming our kids. The best thing we can do is offer gentle words of encouragement, promising things will be better next time.

Encouraging phrases:

"Next time, you will manage to get to the potty faster, that is all right"

"You forgot to tell me that you need to go, next time you will remember"

"You got distracted while playing, let's clean up together and get back to having fun"

Praising our children for something obvious might not be easy at first, but we must do it. With the right encouragement, your daughter will develop the necessary confidence to pursue potty training. She will begin to wait for your praise, as she needs to know that you are proud of what she has achieved so far.

If you are not comfortable with uttering praise out loud, it might not be a bad idea to do some practice. Repeat the encouraging phrases a few times in front of the mirror, and only then utter them to your toddler. Your words should always reflect specific actions the child has achieved, so they facilitate additional progress.

CONCLUSION

As parents, we are lucky to accompany our children in their magical journey of childhood. We get to watch them taking their first step, saying their first word, and yes, using the potty. To be successful with any kind of training, you have to believe in the process. It can be easy to get discouraged, but I encourage you to always find the power to go on.

The three-day potty training method is intense, but it works. Treat the process with earnestness, and keep reminding yourself of the ultimate goal: saying goodbye to diapers. Sure, you will have to ask your daughter over and over again if she needs to pee or poop. At some point, you might begin to hate the sound of your own voice. You will be tired and stressed, and sick of cleaning up. However, knowing that your little one will become more independent, will all be worth it.

Prepare yourself with everything necessary, and do not forget to stock up on underwear. Work on your mental state and do what it takes to maintain a positive attitude. Acknowledge the effort your little one is making, and how hard it can be to leave the diaper behind. Refrain from using harsh words or criticism, as these are not part of a gentle approach, and they can hurt your daughter's soul.

If you are noticing that your little girl is not progressing as expected, showing signs of stress or pressure, take a break. Try to create a relaxed atmosphere, in which she will feel comfortable to try again. Keep in mind that each child is different, and even though this method is pretty straightforward, a more gradual approach might deliver better results. Permit yourself to try various approaches until you find the one that fits the best.

During the training period, make an effort to stay calm and confident. Remember our little ones are always watching us, following our lead. Offer plenty of encouragement and praise, and let your daughter know how proud you are. This is just the beginning and you have a long road ahead; just be patient and help your child go through any challenge. Should a regression occur, work on the root cause and do not hurry your little one back to the potty. Patience is key, first and foremost.

A psychologist might be able to help you, should your toddler refuse to try potty training altogether, even after an extended time of trying. Together, you can explore the emotional issues associated with the refusal and determine if the root cause is a power struggle or something else. For instance, stubborn children are highly likely to refuse to use the potty, so a therapist might teach you how to work on this issue first.

If you had a positive experience with the three-day potty training method, do not hesitate to share your story with other parents. You can recommend them this book to them and offer advice from your point of view.

Printed in Great Britain
by Amazon

37422250R00030